TEENS IN FRANCE

Teens in France

by Nickie Kranz

Content Adviser: Jean-Philippe Mathy, Ph.D.,
Department of French,
University of Illinois at Urbana-Champaign

Reading Adviser: Katie Van Sluys, Ph.D.,
Department of Teacher Education,
DePaul University

Compass Point Books ◆ Minneapolis, Minnesota

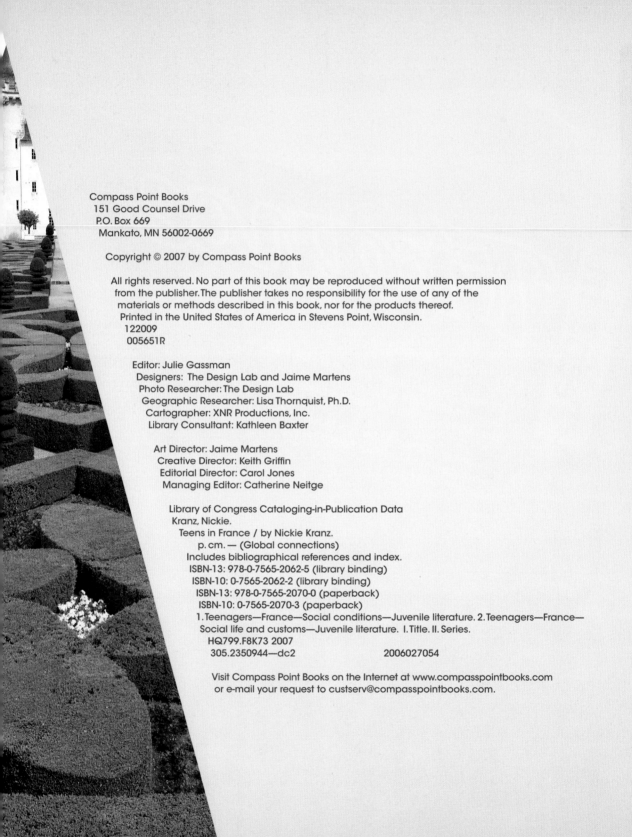

Compass Point Books
151 Good Counsel Drive
P.O. Box 669
Mankato, MN 56002-0669

122009
005651R

Editor: Julie Gassman
Designers: The Design Lab and Jaime Martens
Photo Researcher: The Design Lab
Geographic Researcher: Lisa Thornquist, Ph.D.
Cartographer: XNR Productions, Inc.
Library Consultant: Kathleen Baxter

Art Director: Jaime Martens
Creative Director: Keith Griffin
Editorial Director: Carol Jones
Managing Editor: Catherine Neitge

Library of Congress Cataloging-in-Publication Data
Kranz, Nickie.
Teens in France / by Nickie Kranz.
     p. cm. — (Global connections)
Includes bibliographical references and index.
ISBN-13: 978-0-7565-2062-5 (library binding)
ISBN-10: 0-7565-2062-2 (library binding)
ISBN-13: 978-0-7565-2070-0 (paperback)
ISBN-10: 0-7565-2070-3 (paperback)
1. Teenagers—France—Social conditions—Juvenile literature. 2. Teenagers—France—
Social life and customs—Juvenile literature. I. Title. II. Series.
   HQ799.F8K73 2007
     305.2350944—dc2   2006027054

Visit Compass Point Books on the Internet at www.compasspointbooks.com
or e-mail your request to custserv@compasspointbooks.com.

Table of Contents

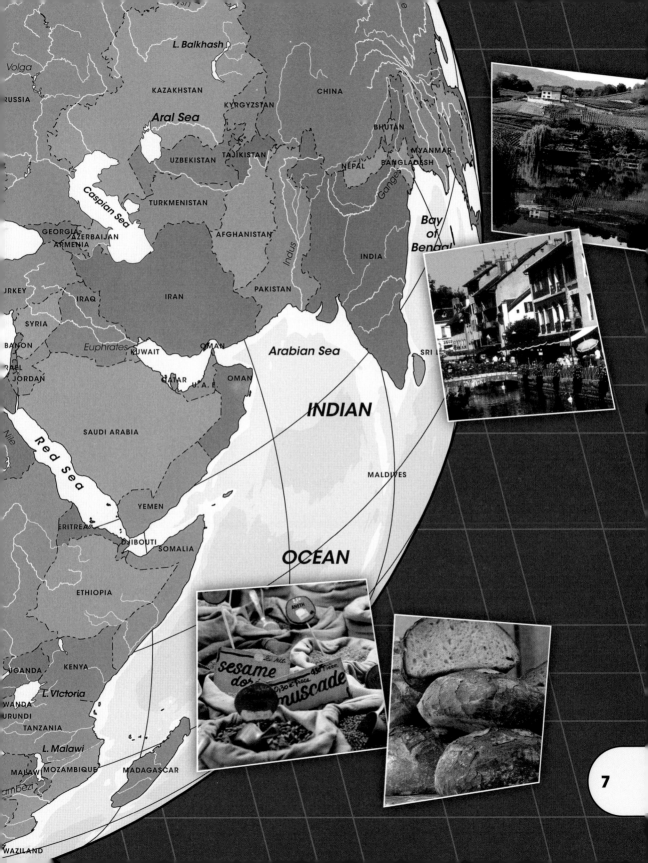

Volga

L. Balkhash

KAZAKHSTAN

KYRGYZSTAN

CHINA

Aral Sea

UZBEKISTAN

TAJIKISTAN

BHUTAN

MYANMAR

NEPAL

BANGLADESH

TURKMENISTAN

Caspian Sea

GEORGIA

AZERBAIJAN

ARMENIA

AFGHANISTAN

Ganges

Bay
of
Bengal

Indus

INDIA

JRKEY

IRAQ

IRAN

PAKISTAN

SYRIA

Euphrates

KUWAIT

OMAN

Arabian Sea

SRI L

BANON

RAEL

JORDAN

QATAR

OMAN

U. A. E.

Nile

Red Sea

SAUDI ARABIA

INDIAN

YEMEN

MALDIVES

ERITREA

DJIBOUTI

SOMALIA

OCEAN

ETHIOPIA

UGANDA

KENYA

WANDA

L. Victoria

URUNDI

TANZANIA

L. Malawi

MALAWI

MOZAMBIQUE

MADAGASCAR

ambezi

WAZILAND

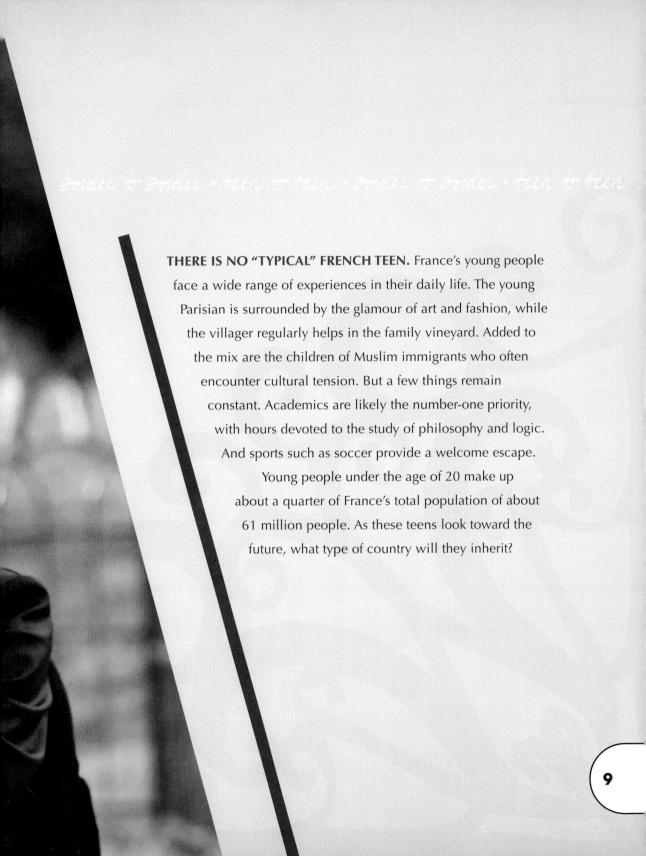

THERE IS NO "TYPICAL" FRENCH TEEN. France's young people face a wide range of experiences in their daily life. The young Parisian is surrounded by the glamour of art and fashion, while the villager regularly helps in the family vineyard. Added to the mix are the children of Muslim immigrants who often encounter cultural tension. But a few things remain constant. Academics are likely the number-one priority, with hours devoted to the study of philosophy and logic. And sports such as soccer provide a welcome escape. Young people under the age of 20 make up about a quarter of France's total population of about 61 million people. As these teens look toward the future, what type of country will they inherit?

In France, high school, or lycée, lasts three years.

1

Formal Learning

IT'S SATURDAY MORNING, AND A FRENCH CLASSROOM IS FILLED WITH TEENAGE STUDENTS. They all listen intently as their teacher presents a lecture on the 1789 storming of the Bastille prison in Paris—an event that began the French Revolution.

While at school, students are focused on one thing: academics. For French teens, sports, clubs, and dances all take place outside of the school system, so time spent in school is time spent in the classroom.

With so much emphasis placed on academics, it is no surprise that students feel driven from an early age to study hard and to do well on exams. Education in France is very formal, very structured, and very competitive.

Teen Scenes

A teenage boy is waiting outside his school in Bordeaux, a southwestern French city, for his mom to pick him up and take him home. Home is about a 30-minute drive away—a family vineyard, which his father runs. The land and the farmhouse have been in their family for 200 years. Once home, the young man will study and listen to some music he downloaded from the Internet earlier. Evening plans include eating dinner and helping his dad in the office to earn his allowance and to learn farm management skills. His plans are to go to college, and then to return home to help run the vineyard.

A girl in the rainy city of Nantes, in the west of France, decides to take the bus home from school to escape another rainy day. As soon as she takes her seat, she text-messages a friend to make plans to see a film and go shopping on Saturday. But she's not even sure if her mom will let her go out on Saturday. She has end of the year exams next week, and her mom will most likely insist that she stay home and study all weekend.

A teen Muslim girl is walking home from school. Her parents came to France before she was born. Her dad has had a good job ever since they immigrated. But she is friends with other second-generation Muslims whose fathers have been unable to get well-paying jobs. Those families live in a nearby rundown project area. When the girl gets home, she takes off her head veil, which she wears when she is around unrelated boys or grown men. Sometimes non-Muslims tease her for wearing it, but their comments do not bother her. When she has it on, people cannot judge her by her appearance. They must judge her by her personality instead—and she likes it that way.

These scenes are a glimpse of the varied lives of teens in France. Different cultural backgrounds create different experiences for the country's youth. However, France's education system brings them together, preparing them to attend college or enter the workforce.

Who's This Descartes Guy?

René Descartes was a scientist, mathematician, and philosopher. He made important contributions to the study of geometry and algebra. His work in philosophy—the study of the nature of reality, matter, knowledge, or life—earned him the title "father of modern philosophy." Descartes is acknowledged for making the development of modern science possible. He used the principles of scientific thinking in his search for truth. For Descartes, the only truths that existed were based on reason, not tradition. For example, he used scientific methods to question people's beliefs in religion and government.

Logic & Philosophy

The French educational system has deep roots, dating back 400 years to the French philosopher René Descartes (1596–1650). Then and now, teachers place the greatest emphasis on logic, philosophy, and debate. They expect students to develop the ability to memorize, think clearly, and discuss abstract ideas.

During a typical school day, students study standard subjects like math, science, and literature; but France may be the only country that requires its high school students to demonstrate an understanding of philosophy. In order to graduate, a student may have to answer questions such as, "Can demands for justice be separated from demands for liberty?" "Do passions prevent us from doing our duty?" The complicated, but thought-provoking, questions require philosophical answers.

These challenging concepts require teens to devote at least a few hours per day studying. One French girl describes

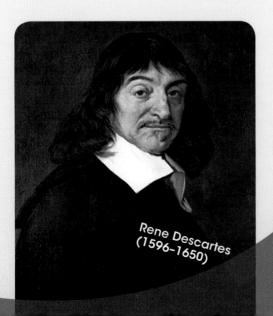

Rene Descartes
(1596–1650)

French School Levels

School Level	Grades	Ages
Pre-elementary		3–5
Primary	1–5	6–11
Collège	6–9	11–15
Lycée	10–12	15–18

The lycée Charlemagne was once the home of a religious order. The school was started in 1804 by Napoléon Bonaparte.

the pressures of her school: "We have a big test every two weeks and a small test every week."

A "small" test, in fact, takes an hour or two, while a "big" test takes up to four hours. At the end of each school year, a student's progress is assessed to determine if the student can proceed to the next grade. According to the Embassy of France in the United States, "teachers give their opinions in what is known as a 'class council,' formed of representatives of pupils, teachers, and parents."

School counselors can help the students and their parents decide if they should appeal any decision the council makes.

School Schedule

Teens in France live with significant stress from their studies, but most schools' schedules are designed to alleviate some of the pressure. Classes are in session all day Monday, Tuesday, Thursday, and Friday, with Wednesdays off to give students a break. The trade-off to having Wednesdays off, though, is that they attend school on Saturday mornings.

Until recently, all French schools followed this schedule. The majority of mothers either did not work outside the home, or they worked part time and were able to be home with their children on Wednesdays. However, because 78 percent of married mothers now work outside the home full time, finding day care on Wednesdays has become a challenge.

Schools are starting to change to a Monday through Friday schedule. Many students who attend schools with the traditional schedule are also hoping their schools will change to this new schedule so that they don't have to get up early on Saturday mornings.

The Day to Day

On days when class is in session, teens get up around 7 A.M. and eat a quick breakfast of biscotti or toast with butter or jam and coffee with milk.

Dressing for school can be a bit of an event in itself, especially for girls. France is known as the world's center of fashion. Young women grow up surrounded with messages that call their attention to trends in clothing, hairstyles, and makeup. Most teenage girls enjoy wearing stylish clothes and makeup to school and want to make sure they are in fashion.

Boys are usually fashion-conscious, too. For example, no boy or girl would

Working mothers can place young children in a crèche, a type of nursery school where they will be cared for as well as educated.

ever wear sweatpants to class.

A policy of the French government has greatly affected the dress at school for some students. In 2004, a law banning students from wearing religious symbols in public schools was passed. This law prohibited Christian students from visibly wearing a cross and Jewish students from wearing a yarmulke, for example. Government leaders believed the policy would help public schools become a melting pot, where differences vanish while students are there.

The law, though, is a major problem for Muslim girls who cover their hair, ears, and neck with a *hijab* in accordance with Islamic law. While their religion asks them to wear this scarf, their school and country forbid them to do so.

hijab
HEE-jib

In order to comply with the law banning religious symbols, many Muslim girls remove their scarves upon entering the school building. They promptly put them on again after school.

Cultural Tension

By far, the largest group of immigrants to France in recent years has been Muslims, most of whom have come from Algeria, a former French colony. Algerians and other North African people make up approximately 80 percent of the immigrants living in France.

Muslims have found it difficult to assimilate into French society. Tensions exist between these immigrants and the native-born French because of racial and cultural differences. Also, native-born French tend to blame these immigrants for the country's high unemployment rate. Although born in France, children of Muslim immigrants often experience racism—even though they speak French and are French-educated.

In October 2005, the frustration of young Muslims came to a head when riots broke out in Paris suburbs. The riots were triggered by the deaths of two teenagers, one of whom was Muslim, living in the impoverished area of Clichy-sous-Bois. The two boys had been playing football with friends when they saw the police approaching. All of the kids fled in different directions. They wanted to avoid identification checks and lengthy questioning from the police, which area youths say they often face. Three of the boys hid in a power substation, and all three of them were electrocuted, two of them to death.

The riots raged for nearly two weeks before President Jacques Chirac declared a state of emergency on November 8.

On October 29, 2005, youths took part in a silent march in memory of the two teens who died. Their shirts read, "Dead for Nothing."

When the law was first passed, girls faced expulsion if they refused to remove their scarves. Two sisters, Alma and Lila, were surprised when school administrators asked them to leave school after they refused to remove their hijabs as their teacher had asked. "We were prepared to have a difficult time," Alma told an interviewer, "but not to that point, honestly!"

Private Schools

Private schools, which follow the same national curriculum as public schools, have an enrollment of about 15 percent of France's primary students and 20 percent of the secondary students. The majority of private schools are denominational, including Catholic, Protestant, Jewish, and Islam. There are also nondenominational private schools, which are boarding schools. Both the denominational and nondenominational schools receive some funding from the government, with the exception of Islam schools, none of which receives federal funding.

Today the law is somewhat flexible, allowing religious symbols as long as the school continues to function as usual. The principal of each school is permitted to decide whether the scarf can be worn. Some principals have no objection to it; others refuse to allow it.

On to School

Once dressed and ready to go, teens will either walk, catch a ride from a parent, or take a bus to school. Most cities have bus systems that serve the city and surrounding villages. The buses serve simultaneously as a school bus and a passenger bus, so students are likely to ride alongside adults who are traveling to or from work.

At school, the young people typically dive into morning classes such as history, math, and English. Students join their parents at home for a two-hour lunch break, where they enjoy a nice meal and relax. Even though teens are likely to have some homework from their morning classes, they will not do the homework over lunch because this time is set aside for relaxation.

After eating with their families, they may get on the computer to download some music, browse through magazines to catch up on the latest trends, or, if they have cell phones, text-message their friends.

Following the two-hour lunch break, afternoon classes may include

The Franco-German History Manual was co-published by the two European nations. The textbook's goal was to give senior high school students a more balanced view of history.

subjects such as German, science, health, and computer science. At all French schools, it is mandatory that students learn two foreign languages. They are able to choose from Spanish, German, and English, the most popular choice.

The French language is the focus of one of the most important classes for young people: language arts. Here students concentrate on speaking and writing in a precise and proper manner. Written French is very formal and the focus is on grammar, spelling, and punctuation, in addition to the ideas being expressed.

French was the language of international relations from the 16th to the early 20th centuries. During this time, regional dialects or languages called *patois* were banned, and children were beaten at school for speaking them.

The idea of French language purity continues today. Established in 1635, the Académie Française is a private organization

patois
PAT-wah

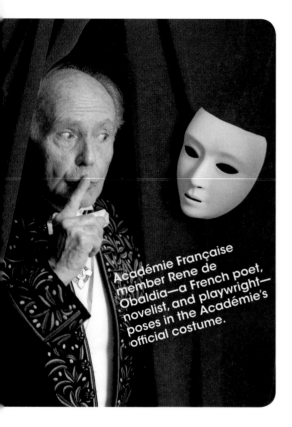

Académie Française member Rene de Obaldia—a French poet, novelist, and playwright—poses in the Académie's official costume.

baladeur
bal-a-duhr
lagiciel
luh-zhee-see-el

At the Diderot Vocational School in Marseille, students learn to make cabinets.

that is responsible for the protection of the French language. This organization publishes the official French dictionary, known as the *Dictionnaire de l'Académie*. It is France's official authority on the usages, vocabulary, and grammar of the language, although its recommendations carry no legal power.

This organization works to ensure academic and political institutions are upholding the correct use of the original language and fights against the French use of slang and imported words, especially in the media. The

Académie tries to prevent English words from being used in the French language. For example, the Académie has replaced the English words of Walkman and software with *baladeur* and *logiciel.*

The Heat is On

Adding to the pressure of challenging classes is the requirement that young people choose between the vocational track and the academic track once they turn 15 and enter *lycée,* or high school.

lycée
lee-SAY

Teens who do not plan to attend college begin training for a specific career in the vocational track. They may do an internship with a business or an apprenticeship with a craftsman to learn a trade such as hairdresser, child care provider, carpenter, or seamstress.

About 61 percent of teens pursue the academic track and prepare to take the baccalaureate exam, a requirement to get into college. In the 11th grade, students on the academic track also choose a specialization from areas such as literature, math, economics, and management. In each specialization, certain classes take up more hours in the weekly schedule than others.

10th Grade Subjects

As 10th graders, all French teens take basically the same classes, no matter what track or specialization they pursue. These include:

French literature
Two foreign languages
History
Geography
Math
Physics
Chemistry
Biology
Economics

Higher Education

Higher education in France is separated into two categories: public university and *grandes écoles.* Since education is paid for by the state, students have an excellent opportunity to receive an education. Grandes écoles are higher education establishments outside the public system. These schools are more selective about admittance and are responsible for producing most of France's scientists and executives. Only about 4 percent of France's students are admitted into grandes écoles. At most grandes écoles tuition is minimal. The exception is business schools where fees runs 6,300 to 7,900 euros (U.S.$8,000 to $10,000).

grandes écoles
graand-zay-kohl

Most of the questions on the baccalaureate exam are given in essay format. The test takes place in June.

A perfect score on the baccalaureate exam is a 20. A student who scores above a 10 is entitled to enroll in one of France's 77 universities. At the public universities tuition is covered by the federal government—a privilege afforded by the high taxes.

The exam is a symbolic part of French culture because it is a rite of passage into adulthood. After the exam is taken, parents throw a huge party, inviting friends and family to the celebration to congratulate the student.

After the first year of college is completed, students have to take an exam before they are allowed to go on to the second year. Only 30 percent to 40 percent of first-year college students pass this exam and go on to the second year of college.

The city of Aix-en-Provence encompasses the love of art, history, and academic achievement for which France is known.

2 The Finer Things in Life

WHETHER A TEEN'S HOME IS IN THE CITY, THE SUBURBS, OR THE COUNTRY, certain aspects of daily life are often the same. Fresh food, fine fashions, and family pets are likely to be part of a French teen's world.

The international impression of France is that its people enjoy life and live it fully. Photographs of France are often filled with women in cutting edge fashion, tables of gourmet food and fine wines, or friends simply relaxing.

These images capture the essence of French lifestyles. The daily activities of France's young people often center on the appreciation of the finer things in France and life in general.

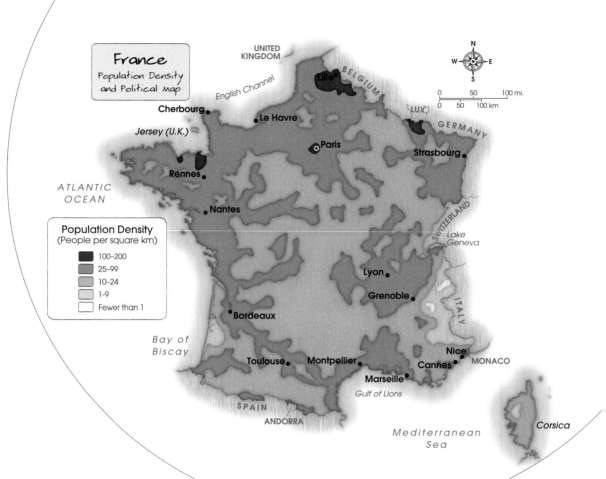

France
Population Density and Political Map

UNITED KINGDOM

English Channel

BELGIUM

Cherbourg

Le Havre

LUX.

Jersey (U.K.)

GERMANY

Paris

Strasbourg

Rennes

ATLANTIC OCEAN

Nantes

SWITZERLAND

Lake Geneva

Population Density
(People per square km)

- 100–200
- 25–99
- 10–24
- 1–9
- Fewer than 1

Lyon

Grenoble

ITALY

Bordeaux

Bay of Biscay

Nice

Toulouse
Montpellier
Cannes
MONACO

Marseille

SPAIN

Gulf of Lions

ANDORRA

Mediterranean Sea

Corsica

N
W E
S

0   50   100 mi.
0   50   100 km

Urban Living

About 80 percent of French people make their homes in towns or bustling cities such as Paris, Marseille, and Lyon. Apartment living is the norm throughout the country—where almost 40 percent of the housing units are apartments, in buildings that are four or five stories high.

The main doors that face the city streets often open up to a courtyard, where elevators or staircases access the higher floors. Security measures, such as a code lock on the street entrance door, are common. Residents and visitors must

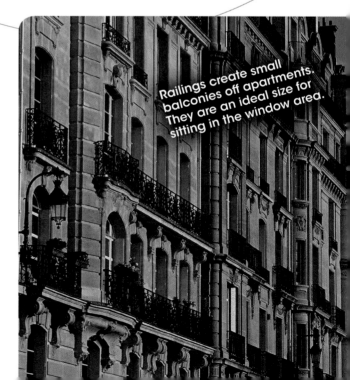

Railings create small balconies off apartments. They are an ideal size for sitting in the window area.

THE FINER THINGS IN LIFE

A man shops in an area called "La Cité des 4,000." Unemployment rates in the area are around 24 percent and even higher among the youth.

know the code, which is changed regularly, if they want to enter the courtyard after 8 P.M.

The older the apartment building, the more expensive and prestigious are the apartments inside. The wealthiest people often live in the city centers, while middle-income residents will commute to jobs in the city from surrounding suburbs.

Teens from lower-income families may live in subsidized housing just outside the urban centers of some cities. In the 1950s, the French government established a program to provide housing at lower prices to those in need. Today about a quarter of the population lives in some form of subsidized housing. These neighborhoods are often marked by high unemployment and poverty rates.

Getting Away

Approximately 3 million households in France own a vacation home, and France has more second-home owners than anywhere else in the world. The second home is most commonly in the country, and city-dwelling owners use their rural houses as places to escape urban living on the weekends. This is considered an age-old French tradition.

The stone homes and buildings in French villages are likely to be centuries old.

Country Life

Families in villages or the country most often live in houses. Rural teens are more likely to have their own bedrooms than their urban contemporaries. Seventeen-year-old Dimitri Naissant has his own room in his family's home in a country village in western France. He describes his home:

"Our house is about 200 years old and is made of stone. The roofs are still constructed using Roman tiles, which have been used for centuries to keep out the rain. We sometimes have huge summer rainstorms called orages, *but the old tiles keep out the wet. In the basement of the house is the cave where we make Pineau de Charentes [a type of alcohol]. It's made with fresh grape juice, which is stopped from fermenting by adding brandy spirit."*

orages
oh-RAZH

Behind the Wheel

Teens can drive at age 16 if a parent is in the vehicle with them. Two years later, they are eligible to get their driver's license, but the test is rigorous. Many applicants do not pass the first time. The test has been made harder and includes a physical exam, because the government is trying to lower the high number of motorist fatalities caused by poor driving. Roadblocks are a common sight. These require a motorist to stop and display a license, proof of insurance, and the vehicle's title. An absence of any one of these three documents can mean immediate arrest. Usually teens get around by bicycle, bus, or small motorbike.

Whether a family lives in a house or an apartment, the residence is typically quite small, consisting of two bedrooms, one bathroom, and small kitchens with small appliances. Although 80 percent of households own a car, garages are not very common, and the cars are kept on the street.

The French are highly advanced in the area of household electronics. Many houses and apartments have automatic opening/closing doors and windows, garden and indoor plant watering systems, distance controlled heat, and advanced lighting systems.

The Family Pet

A pet often shares the family home, and France has more pets per person than any other country in Europe. Perhaps one reason for this is that they are popular gifts. Nine out of 10 cats and

The French carry small pets with them in backpacks or carriers.

29

half of all dogs in the country were given as gifts. A daily chore for some teens is to walk and feed the family dog, perhaps a German shepherd—the most popular breed—or a poodle, the second favorite.

In Paris, where there are more dogs than children, dog owners are not required to clean up after their pets. City employees ride scooters along the sidewalks and clean up the dog waste with a machine that looks much like a vacuum cleaner.

French people cherish their pets so much that there is even a famous pet cemetery in Asniéres, a suburb of Paris, called the Cimetière des Chiens. The high esteem Parisians have for their dogs or cats can be seen in the cemetery's elaborate monuments, featuring drawings or photos of beloved pets.

Rin Tin Tin

A world-famous dog, Rin Tin Tin, is buried in Cimetière des Chiens. Two months before the end of World War I, American serviceman Lee Duncan found Rin Tin Tin, then a puppy, in a bombed-out kennel in Lorraine, France. Duncan named him after a puppet called Rintintin. This was also a name that French children gave to American soldiers for good luck. After the war ended, Duncan took the puppy to his home in Los Angeles, California. Soon Rin Tin Tin appeared in Warner Brothers movies such as *The Man from Hell's River* and *Where the North Begins*. After Rin Tin Tin died, his body was sent back to his homeland of France to be buried.

Rin Tin Tin could leap more than 13 feet (21 meters).

The cassoulet, a dish featuring beans, sausage, and other meats, is a specialty in Carcassonne, a city in southern France.

Food with Flair

Much of a French teen's time at home is devoted to preparing, savoring, and discussing fine cuisine. From wines and cheeses to pastries and breads, France is known for excellence in food and cooking.

Each region of France features its own specialties using local produce. Teens living along the coasts of the Mediterranean Sea or the Atlantic Ocean regularly feast on seafood dishes. Menus in central France are plentiful in fresh vegetables and fruits, while meat dishes are popular in the north, home to the best grazing land for sheep.

All family members help in the garden. Vegetables commonly grown include potatoes, lettuce, carrots, radishes, and herbs.

Commonly, families grow their own vegetables for health benefits and to avoid the expense of buying them at a market. Even apartment dwellers can raise vegetables on their balconies, terraces, or small rented spaces on the edge of town.

The majority of the upkeep is done by the men of the family, but teens are often responsible for weeding the garden regularly in exchange for allowance. In Dimitri Naissant's family, everyone helps out with the garden. "We grow tomatoes, potatoes, green beans, and leeks. It's enough to keep us going throughout most of the year," he said.

A traditional French meal served at home is an extraordinary event, consisting of several courses. Such a lunch or dinner begins with an aperitif (a glass of water, soda, or alcohol), followed by an appetizer, the main course, a salad, cheese, dessert with coffee, and finally, for the adults, a digestif (a small glass of brandy or other alcohol).

Whether the meal is traditional or quick, there is always plenty of bread, which is eaten throughout the meal but never dunked. Someone who dunks bread into food is seen as displaying terrible manners. There is always salt and pepper on the table, whether dining at home or in a restaurant. But if it is used, it is considered an insult to the chef that the food was not seasoned properly.

Favorite Foods

A 17-year-old describes his favorite dish: *"We eat snails, which are called* cagouilles *in this area [south-western France], not the usual French name:* escargots. *We collect them from the fields and hedgerows after it's been raining. My mum ... puts a hundred or more into a pan with sausage, garlic, tomatoes, and herbs and makes a stew, which fills you up very quickly."*

cagouilles
ka-GOY

escargots
ez-kar-goh

French markets and specialty shops offer a wide variety of cheese.

Meals are a time to sit and talk together, and this helps to maintain the family unit.

Cheese, Bread, & Wine

When high school students arrive home from school hungry and needing a snack, they might reach for a bit of cheese. France is home to 500 varieties of cheese produced at French farms, monasteries, and factories. Certain regions are known for producing certain types of cheese, and many take their names from the villages that first produced them. For example, Camembert is a cow's milk cheese named after a village in Normandy, and Roquefort, aged ewe's milk cheese, was once only produced in Roquefort-sur-Soulzon in south-central France.

France is also famous for its bread, including croissants and baguettes.

Bread is offered at every meal, and typical bakeries have at least 28 types of bread to choose from. French bread goes stale quickly, so it is bought fresh each morning for that day's meals. But if the bread happens to get a little stale, all is not lost. Dipping slices in a milk and egg mixture and then frying it is a tasty way to finish off a loaf.

As with bread, French families buy

Rather than purchase all of their groceries at a supermarket, the French visit individual shops, such as the fish monger.

THE FINER THINGS IN LIFE

Fashion & Flair

In daily life, the average French girl devotes much time and attention to fashion, cosmetics, and hairstyles. Surrounded by some of the best-known fashion labels in the world, including Chanel and Christian Dior, French people typically value style and quality in their clothing.

Young women are taught to present a certain attitude and style in the way they carry themselves. Walking with straight backs and heads held high, the young women display their bravado with boldness, and confidence. Most French girls are slim, and they tend to show disdain for overweight people from other countries. Concerned with their health and body image, they exercise regularly and rarely snack between meals except to have fruit, yogurt, bread, or small amounts of chocolate after school.

Males are usually very polite and display proper French etiquette in social settings. They stand when a woman enters the room, and they open the door to let her through first.

small quantities of other fresh food at a time. Most people shop daily for what they are planning to serve that night. Small grocery stores are very common, with the freshest, most succulent produce available. The quality of France's produce is exceptional.

In large cities, there are open-air markets three times a week that offer produce, meats, cheeses, flowers, and even clothes. Specialty shops are very common, including bakeries, butcher shops, and cheese shops. Today, for a fee, many of these small shops will deliver the grocery orders.

Along with bread, wine is also offered at every meal. The French consider choosing and enjoying fine wine as something of an art. It is imperative that the wine has the right color, smell, and taste to accompany the food that it is being served with. This art is passed down to teens from generation upon generation. The legal drinking age is 16, but younger teens will often enjoy a glass of wine at family dinners.

French Prime Minister Dominique de Villepin runs with his son during a family vacation.

3

The Heart of Society

FAMILY LIFE IS DESCRIBED AS BEING AT THE HEART OF FRENCH SOCIETY. French Prime Minister Dominique de Villepin said this about family: "It is a source of joy, of comfort, and a haven for its members." Teens spend many hours gathered around the family dinner table and many weekends enjoying their family's company.

French families take all sorts of shapes. The number of births per woman is one or two, resulting in small families. Currently, 17 percent of all households in France are single-parent households. And about 46 percent of births in 2004 occurred outside of marriage. But no matter what a family's makeup, it is likely a source of love and pride for people young and old.

French children continue to live at home much longer than children

What's In a Name
Popular names in France

For Boys

Baptiste
Clement
Enzo
Hugo
Leo
Louis
Lucas
Matheo
Theo
Thomas

For Girls

Anais
Camille
Chloe
Clara
Emma
Jade
Lea
Luci
Manon
Marie

in other industrialized nations. Those who attend college will most likely choose the university that is closest to home. About 73 percent of students between the ages of 15 and 24 live at home with their parents, and they often don't move out until they get married.

Even after moving to their own homes, young people usually stay in close contact with their parents. The family unit is not a separate part of a teenager's life, but rather a very important part that plays a large role in the decisions teenagers make in

Because families tend to be physically close, young children often have close relationships with their grandparents.

To support larger families, the government has funded projects like Paris' Cafezoide—a day care, cultural center, and cafe that helps parents meet other parents in the neighborhood.

virtually all areas of their lives.

Families in France seldom move, so it is very common for parents, their married children, and members of the extended family to all live near each other. The French take pride in the job of providing support for their relatives.

Like its citizens, the government holds family in high esteem and actively works to encourage families to have more than two children. Incentives such as government money for mothers who take time off from work to have a third child, as well as funding to help with day care expenses, are designed to ensure that larger families are not strained. Hubert Brin, president of the National Union of Family Associations, believes these incentives are extremely important because "spending on young children is spending on the future of France."

A Look at Family Life

Life is busy in France, with both parents often working and teenage children consumed with their schoolwork. But parents try to stay involved with their children's school and home lives. They make sure to know what the students are studying and help regularly with homework, which can take several hours each night to complete.

While teens learn instruction at school, they learn social rules at home. Parents have the responsibility of training their children to become, responsible citizens and to teach them the importance of conforming to the rules of French society. Just as the academic expectations are high, so are the standards of social behavior.

In France, etiquette is extremely important and must be observed at all times. For example, the French people shake hands on arriving and leaving, even at work and school. If a teenager meets a group of friends in a coffee shop, it is normal to shake hands with everybody in the group. The tradition of shaking hands comes from an age-old French tradition that proved you were not holding a dagger.

Dinners are important times for families to gather and discuss their days.

Polite & Proper

Even with informal conversation, you may insult someone by not addressing him or her correctly. For example, adding "sir" or "madam" is correct behavior. Omitting either is not only incorrect, it is also considered extremely rude. When greeting an adult, a teenager should say "Bonjour, Monsieur" or "Bonjour, Madame," not just "Bonjour."

In subsidized housing in the impoverished suburbs, family communication has suffered. The problem is often caused by frustrations over unemployment.

Parents push their children to do better both academically and socially with statements such as "That's not good enough. I know you can do better." They aim to raise their children to be model family members and citizens who will conform to French society.

In French culture the group is valued more than the individual, and building a social identity is much more important than encouraging self-expression. The French believe that certain basic attitudes and values need to be taught and followed. The French worry that not adhering to their social rules and values could lead to a breakdown in society and threaten the traditional French way of life.

When eating at the table, for example, parents criticize bad behavior and careless remarks. Children are told that if they are going to say something, it needs to be either witty or intelligent. French teens will very rarely raid the fridge, forget to clean their rooms, borrow the car without permission, or talk back to adults. These things are not permitted. If rules are disobeyed in public, parents will reprimand their children verbally and sometimes even physically with a slap. But French parents also openly show affection, kissing and hugging their children in public.

While committed to the formation of strong social identities, French families are also private. Only the closest of friends are invited to family gatherings, and therefore an invitation is considered a privilege. The importance of family is seen at the national level also. France prefers to be thought of as a national family, joined together by history, experience, and language.

Time for Friends

Between their vigorous studies and dedicated family life, if might seem like

Street Slang

A new slang language is starting to get under the skin of parents throughout France. Spoken among teen friends, the language is known as Verlan. It is a mix of French, English, and Arabic words. In addition, speakers often take a French word and reverse the syllables. Bizarre, for example, becomes *zarbi*.

To the horror of the Académie Française, Verlan is turning up everywhere—schools, newspapers, movies, and music. Verlan has grown to consist of hundreds of words. Adults cannot keep up with it because many words are changed as soon as mainstream society figures out their meanings.

One 16-year-old boy was asked how often he uses Verlan in a typical day. He replied, "A lot. Ten thousand times." What do his parents think? "They say it makes me sound like a moron."

Though the French business world was slow to warm up to text-messaging, the country's youth embraced the technology.

French teens do not have much time for friends. But they are able to carve out time here and there to just hang out with their peers. On school days, a two-hour lunch break provides the opportunity to text-message friends.

According to one former French student, text-messaging is very common with teens in France, and many young people have a cell phone by the time they are 12 or 13 years old. Text-messaging is the only way to communicate with friends during the school day because teachers strictly prohibit talking in class.

Saturday afternoons are a good time for teens to get together. They commonly meet at coffee shops first and decide where to go or what to do from there. Girls enjoy window shopping with friends, and both boys and girls enjoy athletic activities, such as cycling or downhill skiing, depending on the season. Catching an afternoon movie is also popular with both boys and girls.

In cities, public transportation like Paris' metro system, makes it easy for teens to get around.

The Money Gap

While many French teens are able to enjoy the technologies of cell phones and personal computers, not all are so lucky. Even though France has one of the strongest economies in Europe, about 12 percent of the population is considered to be poor because of the high levels of unemployment. The gap between the rich and the poor is wider in France than in any other European nation. The top 1 percent of the French own 20 percent of the country's private wealth, while the bottom 10 percent of the French own only 0.1 percent of the wealth. For example, it is not uncommon for the average business manager to make seven times as much as his or her employees.

Young men and women who are dating most often go out with groups of friends or each other's families. Favorite activities include attending movies or concerts or hanging out at cafés.

In Paris, Bastille Day brings a sky filled with fireworks.

4

Festivities in France

AS A CULTURE THAT VALUES FINE FOOD, WINE, AND TIME WITH FRIENDS AND FAMILY, it is no surprise that the French fill their year with holidays and celebrations. Holidays such as Bastille Day, World War II Victory Day, and Armistice Day are patriotic in nature, while others, such as Noël (Christmas), have religious roots. In addition, many communities throughout France hold festivals during the year that celebrate music, dance, wine, and films.

Birthdays, weddings, and other personal events create even more excuses for teens to cut loose and celebrate. Here is a look at a few of the most popular celebrations for French teens.

Public Holidays

Jour de l'An (New Year's Day)—January 1	
Pâques (Easter)—March/April	
Fête du Travail (Labor Day)—May 1	
Lundi de Pentecôte (Whit Monday)—May	
Victoire 1945 (World War II Victory Day)—May 8	
Fête Nationale (Bastille Day)—July 14	
Assomption (Assumption of the Blessed Virgin)—August 15	
Toussaint (All Saints Day)—November 1	
Armistice Day—November 11	
Noël (Christmas)—December 25	
New Year's Eve—December 31	

For Love of Country

France's national holiday, Bastille Day, celebrates the day of July 14, 1789, when rebellious Parisians stormed the Bastille prison. This is the act that began the French Revolution, which eventually pushed out the ruling monarchy and established a republic.

Honoring Heroes

Two of France's public holidays honor the heroes of war. Armistice Day, on November 11, is a tribute to the soldiers who served in World War I. It commemorates the day in 1918 when the Allies and Germany signed the agreement that ended the four-year war.

On May 8, the veterans of World War II are honored on Victoire 1945 (World War II Victory Day). More than

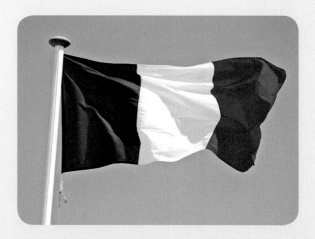

560,000 French soldiers and civilians lost their lives in the war, and much of the country was devastated.

This day is celebrated with parades, music, and dancing throughout France and even other areas of the world. In Paris, the French president attends the city's military parade down Paris' most famous street, the Champs-Elysées. Cadets from several universities start the parade, followed by the infantry and other troops. But the crowd favorite is the fire brigade, the city's firefighters who are often tired from a full night of parties on the holiday's eve. After the parade, the president gives a televised interview.

Parents often let their teens stay out late on July 14 so the young people can take part in the local street dance. With music, dancing, champagne, and fireworks, each Bastille Day is one to remember.

French military members parade past the Arc de Triomphe during the Bastille Day parade in Paris. The massive monument was commissioned in 1806 by Napoléon Bonaparte.

49

For Music Lovers

As a cultural leader, France is a trend-setter in many ways. Fête de la Musique, a national music festival, is one example. Since France first held Fête de la Musique on June 21, 1982, countries all over the world—including Egypt, Cambodia, Congo, and Chile, to name just a few—have joined in the fun.

Back in 1982, leaders in the Ministry of Culture wanted to encourage both amateur and professional musicians to get out and play, for at least one day. Event organizers knew that the French owned more than 4 million musical instruments, but the vast majority of these instruments were stored away in attics, closets, and cellars. This question,

The Palace of Versailles serves as a backdrop for large concerts held on Fête de la Musique. Now a museum, the palace was the official home of the French kings from 1682 to 1790.

Musical acts are incredibly varied, including performances by solo percussionists.

later written down by an adviser in the Ministry of Culture, spurred the event:

"Why couldn't, one day a year, those cellos, guitars, trombones, kettledrums, triangles and big bass drums wake up, be restored, produce sounds, find someone to play them and enchant anyone who cared to listen?"

The first year of the festival was a great success, with 79 percent of the French population participating as either a listener or musician. Today, 10 million people of all ages turn out to hear about 800,000 performers in the streets, train stations, school playgrounds, cafés, and concert halls. Most performances are free of charge, and the music ranges from jazz and gospel to teen favorites like pop and techno.

'Tis the Season

Of all the religious holidays celebrated in France, Noël, or Christmas, is one of the most popular. Between 83 percent and 88 percent of the population is Roman Catholic. Though most Roman

A charity organization, Emmaus, serves a Le Réveillon meal to about 500 homeless people in a Paris museum.

Catholics do not attend church regularly, many families attend midnight Mass to start their holiday.

Afterward, families share a late-night meal called Le Réveillon either at home or at one of the many restaurants or cafés that stay open late. *Réveillon* means "to wake up or revive" and is symbolic of the coming of Jesus' birth. The traditional meal begins with oysters for an appetizer, turkey, capon (a type of rooster) or goose and a white pudding called *boudin blanc* for the main course, and special cakes for dessert.

Following the meal, it is traditional to leave a candle burning when going

boudin blanc
boo-DAHN blahng

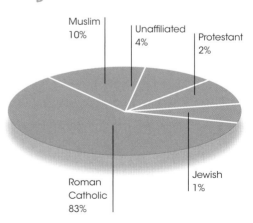

Religions in France

Muslim 10%
Unaffiliated 4%
Protestant 2%
Roman Catholic 83%
Jewish 1%

Source: United States Central Intelligence Agency. *The World Factbook—France.*

Printemps, a favorite Paris department store, is filled with shoppers and is brightly decorated for the holiday season.

crèche
kresh

to bed in case the Virgin Mary passes by. Another holiday tradition is setting up the *crèche*, a type of Nativity scene. The tradition dates back to 1802 and is done in stages beginning on the eve. It is completed on January 6, the Epiphany, when the three kings are added.

Presents are exchanged on Noël or the night before. Teens enjoy using

Celebrate & Honor

Here's a look at a few more holidays that French teens enjoy.

Epiphany—On this religious holiday, which falls on January 6, the three kings who visited the infant Jesus are celebrated. The family buys a crown-shaped cake with a hidden ceramic figure baked inside. The person who gets the slice with the figurine in it is "king or queen for the day" and chooses a royal partner.

Candlemas—February 2 is also known as the Feast of the Virgin and marks the end of the Noël and Epiphany season. Traditionally, pancakes are eaten on this day, but only after 8 P.M. If the cook can flip the pancake while holding a coin in the other hand, the family is ensured good fortune throughout the coming year.

Valentine's Day—Teens enjoy sending flowers to loved ones on February 14.

Easter—On this Christian holiday commemorating the resurrection of Jesus Christ, teens traditionally join their extended family at their grandparents' home for a meal. Chocolate eggs, chocolate chickens, or chocolate rabbits are hidden in the garden for children to find.

Mother's Day and Father's Day—French people began celebrating these spring holidays after World War II. Families gather together, and teens present the honored parent with a gift purchased with allowance money.

Halloween—Traditions such as pumpkins, masks, witches, and ghosts are popular in France on October 31. Even though Halloween traditions began in Europe, Halloween was considered mostly an American holiday until recently. Because of the American influence, some teens spend the night hanging out at an all-American restaurant—McDonald's.

Trocadéro garden in Paris is decorated with 8,000 pumpkins for Halloween.

FESTIVITIES IN FRANCE

their allowance money to purchase gifts for family members and a girlfriend or boyfriend. When shopping during the holiday, a person will see numerous Noël markets with ornaments and cuckoo clocks for sale.

Young children put shoes in front of the fireplace in hopes that they will be filled with gifts by Père Noël, a figure who is the equivalent of Santa Claus. On the night before Noël, it is traditional to decorate the tree with candy, fruit, and nuts. Parents hang small toys on the tree after bedtime. Père Fouettard, another traditional Noël character, gives out spankings to bad children. Père Noël visits the good children, and Père Fouettard visits the bad. Mistletoe is hung above a door throughout the season to bring good luck for the next year.

Père Noël visits some French children twice in December—on December 6 for St. Nicholas Day and December 24 for Christmas Eve.

Celebrating with Family

Teens also look forward to celebrating momentous family events. For example, weddings are large affairs filled with countless French traditions. Whether religious or not, the couple must publish an official marriage notice at least 10 days before the wedding and marry in the town hall to satisfy a national requirement of a civil marriage. Often a religious ceremony is held after the civil ceremony is completed, with family and friends invited.

In many towns, the groom walks the bride from her home to the church for the religious ceremony, while children run alongside the couple. Once at the church, the couple weds under a *carré*. This silk canopy is believed to protect the couple from bad luck. Later, when the couple starts a family,

carré
KAH-ray

Decorating a get-away vehicle is a popular tradition in the old town of Sarlat in the southwestern part of France.

A croquembouche can be decorated with a miniature bride and groom.

Though the reception ends, the celebration does not. It is traditional for friends to join outside the newlyweds' window to shout and bang on pots and pans. The couple willingly invites their disturbers to join them to extend the party a bit longer.

their children will be baptized under the same carré.

At the reception, the wedding cake often takes the form of a *croquembouche*. This pyramid-shaped dessert is formed from crème-filled pastry puffs and drizzled with a caramel glaze. The couple drinks from a toasting cup, called the *coupe de mariage,* which is passed down through the generations.

Happy Birthday!

Another important family celebration for a French teen is a birthday. Young people's birthdays are most often celebrated at home with cake, presents, and family. Of all Europeans, the French spend the most money on birthday gifts. A teenager's 18th birthday is the most significant because this is the age when a French citizen can legally drink and can obtain a driver's license. It is a coming-of-age party.

Future perfumers of all ages and experience can be trained to recognize about 500 scents at a special school in Grasse, just inland from the French Riviera.

5

From Fashion to Farming

WITH SO MUCH IMPORTANCE PLACED ON ACADEMICS, IT IS UNCOMMON FOR TEENAGERS TO HAVE A JOB. In most regions of France, young adults are 18 before they search for work. One French student points out that because of the large amount of homework, they cannot have jobs after school. "We don't have time," she said.

There are a few exceptions, of course. Some older teens may work in the summer in the wine country, but this is more for the experience than for the money. Or if a family owns a small shop, the teen may help there on occasion, but it is not a common occurrence.

Fighting a Youth Labor Law

In March 2006, French Prime Minister Dominique de Villepin crafted a proposal called the Contrat Première Embauche (CPE), or First Employment Contract. The proposal encouraged employers to hire people under the age of 26 under contract, with the understanding that the employers could terminate the contract within two years without cause. Previous policy did not allow employers to terminate employment without provable cause. The prime minister believed CPE would decrease youth unemployment, which was at 23 percent nationwide and more than 50 percent in high-immigration areas.

The proposal angered students and union leaders, who saw the contract as threatening to what little job security they had. They were also upset that de Villepin had taken his proposal straight to Parliament, without informing the public. Millions of people, including union workers and high school and university students, protested in 250 towns and cities all over the country. In some areas, riots and demonstrations became violent. Protesters and police exchanged blows. In Paris alone, more than 4,000 soldiers were deployed to keep the peace. By late March, more than 1,420 people had been arrested.

President Jacques Chirac gave in to protesters on April 10, 2006. A new law was drafted, offering more support for companies that hire young workers and increasing internships in job markets that have consistent openings, such as food service, hotels, and nursing.

A Paris march against the CPE in March 2006 turned violent.

Even though the majority of teens don't have a job, it doesn't mean that they're not thinking about work. Because they are expected to choose between the academic and vocational tracks as 10th graders, teens in France begin thinking about future career choices at a young age.

At Your Service

The majority of teens will enter service industries when they have completed their education, joining more than 71 percent of workers. Fields within this industry include education, health care, retail, and financial services.

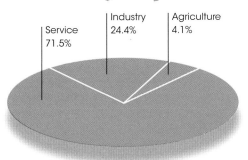

Labor Force by Occupation

Service 71.5%
Industry 24.4%
Agriculture 4.1%

Source: United States Central Intelligence Agency. *The World Factbook—France.*

For the Worker

The Ministry of Employment and Solidarity deals with all questions relating to equal employment opportunities. It strives to ensure equal rights for employees and promotes civil, social, and health rights. The French feel an obligation to help one another, for the good of all. Because of this belief, one of the most powerful positions in the French government is that of the leader of the ministry. In June 1998, the ministry implemented a 35-hour workweek and extended full health care benefits to welfare recipients.

The Seine, a major river in northwestern France, flows past the Cathedral of Notre Dame in Paris.

Also falling under the service umbrella is tourism, an industry that directly employs more than a million people. France is the most popular tourist destination in the world, with more than 75 million visitors each year.

What draws visitors to France? For one, the romantic city of Paris is on many travelers' must-see list. It is home to some of the most famous cultural sites in the world. Top on the list is the Cathedral of Notre Dame, which draws 12 million visitors a year with its breathtaking Gothic architecture. The Eiffel Tower, too, is a major attraction, visited by more than 6 million people each year.

Another draw to France is its natural beauty, featuring some of the most varied topography in all of Europe: the French Alps, the Jura and Pyrénées mountain ranges, agricultural land, canyons, forests, and 2,300 miles (3,680 kilometers) of coastline. The extensive coastline includes the English Channel, the Bay of Biscay, and the Mediterranean Sea. And one of the most beautiful seashores in the world is the French Riviera, which runs along the southeastern coast. With its varied landscape and mild climate, France is considered by many to be the geographical and commercial gateway to all of Europe.

Or Maybe Manufacturing

Some French teens may consider a career in manufacturing industries, which employ another 24 percent of French workers. Together, the manufacturing of items such as automobiles, chemicals, steel, and textiles make France the fourth-ranked manufacturing power in the world, just behind the United States, Japan, and Germany.

Of the manufacturing industries in France, the fashion and luxury goods

Students from all over the world come to study fashion in France, an international leader of the industry.

industry is among the most famed and glamorous. While it employs about 180,000 workers in the country, it reaches the lives of many more all over the world.

France's industry of elegant, high-fashion clothes has historical roots. French designers invented lace, high-heeled shoes, and neckties. In the 1850s, Englishman Charles Worth opened the first known fashion salon in Paris to sell the custom-made high fashions known as haute couture. In the 20th century, French designers including Coco Chanel, Christian Dior, Yves Saint-Laurent, and Pierre Cardin set the world's fashion trends, and their fashion houses continue to do so today.

Money Talk

In 2002, most countries in the European Union replaced their own money—the franc, mark, florin, peseta, lira, schilling, and escudo—with the euro. The euro is now used throughout most of Europe, rather than each country having its own currency. This change has produced great opportunities for economic growth because the euro makes Europe a unified market and a global economic power. It also has made travel from country to country much more convenient; travelers no longer need to exchange currency before entering another country.

FROM FASHION TO FARMING

French Farmers

The remaining 4 percent of French workers are employed in agriculture, helping to make France the leading agricultural country in western Europe. Farms cover about 56 percent of the land, with different areas ideal for different types of farming.

The Paris Basin, located in the north-central part of the country, produces numerous agricultural products. Grains and fruits grow well in this

Teens in farm families help with chores such as checking to ensure that sows do not lie on their piglets.

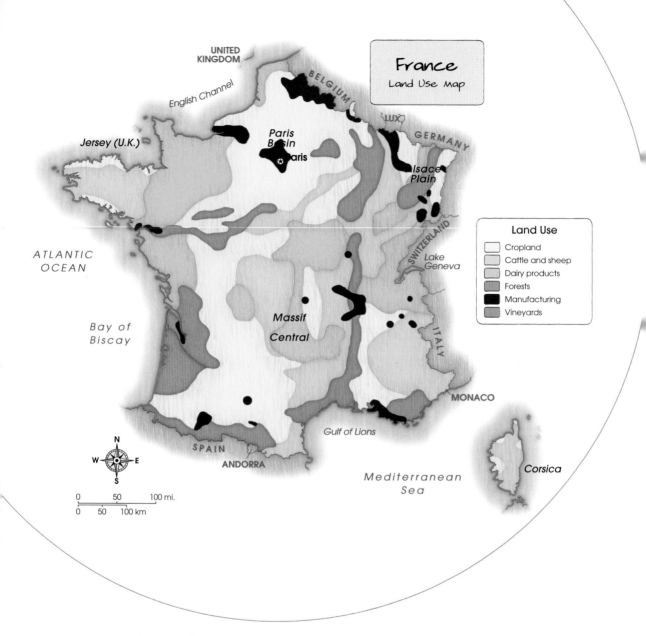

France
Land Use Map

UNITED KINGDOM

English Channel

BELGIUM

LUX.

GERMANY

Jersey (U.K.)

Paris Basin

Paris

Isace Plain

ATLANTIC OCEAN

SWITZERLAND

Lake Geneva

Bay of Biscay

Massif Central

ITALY

MONACO

SPAIN

ANDORRA

Gulf of Lions

Mediterranean Sea

Corsica

Land Use

- Cropland
- Cattle and sheep
- Dairy products
- Forests
- Manufacturing
- Vineyards

N W E S

0   50   100 mi.
0   50   100 km

region's fertile soil. Wheat production is especially important in the area. About 5 percent of the world's wheat is grown in France, and the grain is an important export. Cattle and pigs can be seen grazing troughout the region.

This basin is also home to 25 percent of France's population, mostly because of the appealing temperate climate. The winters are mildly cool, and the summers are long and warm.

The Alsace Plain, which lies just

FROM FASHION TO FARMING

east of the Paris Basin, is known for its many vineyards. The region around the city of Bordeaux is also famous for its vineyards.

The Massif Central range, in the southeast, is the largest area of highland topography in France. Farmers in this area graze sheep and goats and produce corn and vegetables. The climate is much different here than in the Paris Basin. The winters are long and cold, and the summers are short.

From the Grapevine

Wine is this country's top export, and France is second only to Italy in wine production. The Alsace region, located in a lowland basin along the Rhine River, is renowned for its grapes used to make fine white wines. The basin that surrounds the city of Bordeaux is also well-known for its rich vineyards. France produces approximately 1.5 billion gallons (5.7 billion liters) of wine annually.

Chamonix is a popular winter sports resort. Some of the world's best ski runs are found in the area.

6

Active Minds, Active Bodies

THE FRENCH ADMIRE HARD WORK, BUT THEY ARE NOT WORKAHOLICS. The weekend, for example, is reserved for children and most adults to relax, participate in sports, watch sports on television, or hang out with friends or family. Vacationing provides longer getaways for teens and their families, and 60 percent of the population take at least one trip each year.

There is a strong cultural belief that an active mind needs to be balanced with a healthy body. Parents pass on this belief by pursuing cultural and physical activities together with their children. Teens use leisure activities to provide balance in their lives. Active minds come from playing video games, reading magazines and books, and going to the movies, theater, concerts, and museums.

Active bodies enjoy dancing, skiing, cycling, playing soccer, and more. Every year, the average French household spends 1,075 euros (U.S.$1,367) on cultural and leisure activities.

Happy Holidays

Teens and children in France love to get away from home. Seventy-one percent of teens ages 14 to 19 take a holiday, or vacation, each year, often staying with friends or relatives. Traditionally, teens—with or without their families in tow—seldom spent vacations overseas because, according to many French, there is no better place. But that is beginning to change. Now, about one-fourth of people between the ages of 18 and 25 travel out of the country.

Most employed adults have about five weeks of paid vacation time a year. French employers believe that employees are less stressed if they have ample opportunities to take vacations—and less stress equals better job performance. For many French workers, holidays fall in July or August.

When the French vacation in their own country, one activity they

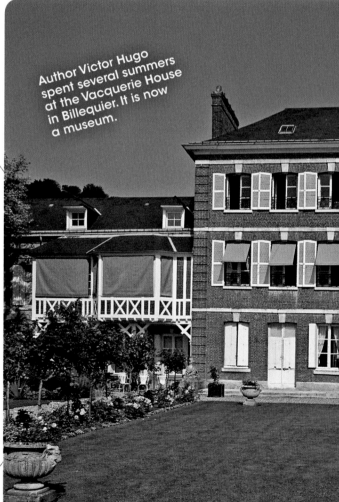

Author Victor Hugo spent several summers at the Vacquerie House in Billequier. It is now a museum.

Top 10 Foreign Vacation Destinations

Country	Percentage of French travelers
Spain	21.2%
Italy	11.7%
Portugal	10.3%
Morocco	8.5%
Tunisia	5.7%
Turkey	4.2%
Algeria	3.8%
Greece	3.7%
United States	3.5%

love is "cultural tourism." They visit places and attend events that involve only French culture and history. A person can visit one of 34 national museums or go on a writers' house tour. These tours include 120 houses that date back to the Renaissance period. They were the homes of France's most famous philosophers and writers.

Famous From France

Many world famous artists, musicians, and writers have hailed from France.

Victor Hugo (1802-1885) Poet and novelist who wrote *The Hunchback of Notre Dame*
Hector Berlioz (1803–1869) Musical composer who wrote *Symphonie Fantastique*
George Bizet (1838–1875) Musical composer who wrote the opera *Carmen*
Claude Monet (1840–1926) Painter and a member of the Impressionist group
Auguste Rodin (1840–1917) French sculptor who created the world famous piece *The Thinker*
Pierre Auguste Renoir (1841–1919) Painter and a founder of the Impressionist group
Claude Debussy (1862–1918) Musical composer who wrote "Clair de Lune"

The French find delight in touring these houses and museums because it enhances their historical knowledge, which can then be used in conversation. For example, rather than talking about what was on television the night before, a teen may ask friends if they have seen the new exhibit at a nearby museum.

Destinations for active vacations are found throughout the country as well. The beaches of the Mediterranean and the Atlantic coasts are hot spots to

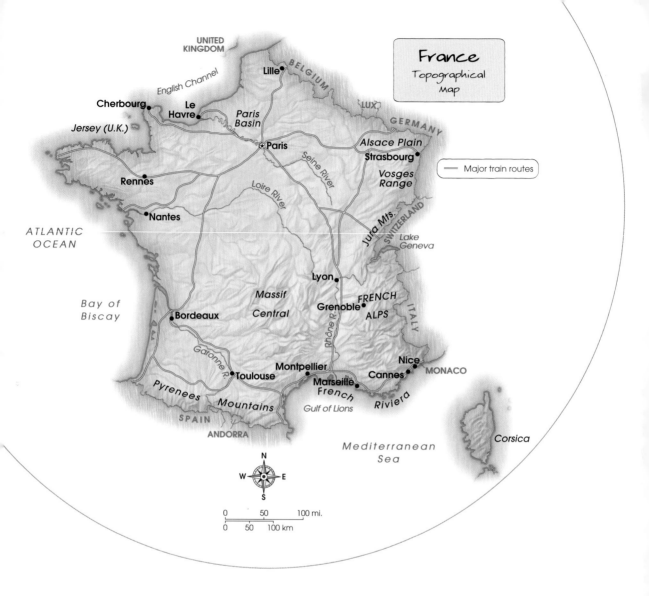

France
Topographical
Map

UNITED KINGDOM

English Channel

BELGIUM

Lille

LUX.

GERMANY

Cherbourg
Le Havre

Paris Basin

Jersey (U.K.)

Paris

Alsace Plain

Strasbourg

Vosges Range

Major train routes

Rennes

Seine River

Loire River

Jura Mts.

SWITZERLAND

Lake Geneva

Nantes

ATLANTIC OCEAN

Lyon

Bay of Biscay

Massif Central

Grenoble

FRENCH ALPS

Bordeaux

Garonne R.

Rhône R.

ITALY

Toulouse

Montpellier

Marseille

French

Nice

Cannes

MONACO

Pyrenees Mountains

Gulf of Lions

Riviera

SPAIN

ANDORRA

Mediterranean Sea

Corsica

N
W E
S

0   50   100 mi.
0   50   100 km

sunbathe, swim, and go kayaking. Many families use some of their five weeks of vacation time in the winter to ski, which is one of the most popular vacation choices for teens. There are 400 ski resorts in the Alps, Jura, Pyrénées, Vosges, and Massif Central mountain areas. French teens are outdoor enthusiasts, and they enjoy picnicking and camping, both of which can be done in the most beautiful places in France.

Since many schools are changing to a Monday through Friday schedule, weekend getaways are becoming more common than in years past. A trip to a theme park makes a great weekend trip,

The French Riviera is part of the southeastern coast off the Mediterranean Sea. It is one of the world's most famous resort areas.

and there are more than 20 theme parks in France, including Disneyland Paris. Its Enchanted Kingdom is the most popular tourist destination in all of Europe, with 12.5 million visitors each year.

School Holidays

Students have a 15-day break for both the Noël (Christmas) and Pâques (Easter) holidays. French teens also enjoy a weeklong break from school each winter. The country is divided into three sections. Each section is given a different week off in winter, sometime between mid-February and mid-March. The school break is staggered to avoid overcrowding at the country's ski resorts.

Daily Getaways

Films, television, radio, and reading are just a few of the ways teens can have fun without leaving town or even home.

More than 34 percent of French people see a movie at least once a month. A popular activity for families with young children is to go to American-made animated films, but the French are famed for their own productions, which display great creative talent. France is the fourth-largest film producer in the world, behind the United States, India, and China. Many films are intelligent and sensitive, focusing on human relationships.

France is home to one of the world's largest annual film festivals. First held in 1946, the Cannes Film Festival began as more of a small attraction for

Attendance at the Cannes Film Festival is limited to film industry professionals.

FESTIVAL DE CANNES
11 MAI - 22 MAI 2005

those who enjoyed film. Over the years it gained popularity and is now considered to be the world's most prestigious and respected film festival.

Held annually in May in southern France's resort town of Cannes, the festival is given massive media exposure because it is attended by famous movie stars and directors. Movie producers show their new films at the festival with the hopes of selling them to film distributors, who come to the festival from all over the world. A variety of films are shown each year, from the unusual and artistic to the commercially popular.

Listening to the radio and watching television are also popular pastimes. On average, the French watch television or listen to the radio six hours a day. Radio France is the public radio system that

Shopping & Sidewalk Cafés

Saturday window shopping is a popular leisure activity with teens. There are very few malls in all of France; most shops are sidewalk shops. Another popular pastime for teens is to sit at a sidewalk café and watch for friends to walk by. The cafés are great meeting places. As long as teens buy coffee, tea, juice, or soda (although soda is rarely ordered), they can sit for as long as they like. Teens like to meet and hang out at McDonald's as well.

broadcasts more than 50 stations, offering everything from a 24-hour news station to jazz to British and American pop.

According to French law, at least 40 percent of the music played on variety stations must consist of songs in the French language. This means that big hits originally sung in English have to be re-recorded in French before they can be played on the radio. Sometimes, the remakes do not translate perfectly, and the finished product ends up being quite humorous.

Teens do not have to rely on the radio to get their music fix. Many

Music Man

One of the most popular raï musicians in France is Cheb Mami. He was born Mohamed Khelifati on July 11, 1966, in Saida, Algeria. From the time he was a child, he was interested in music, and at the age of 12 he became an apprentice raï musician. During the week he helped support his family, but on the weekend he traveled away from Saida and toward the active nightlife of Oran. In 1982, Mami entered a singing competition, and, at a time when Algerian government officials denied the existence of raï music, won second place. A producer heard him, and soon Mami was recording his first album.

His musical style is well-known for combining the traditional music of Algeria with more modern, Western styles like rap, techno, and ska. In 1999, Mami was invited to collaborate on the song "Desert Rose" with British musician Sting, making him an international singing sensation in countries like Algeria, France, Morocco, and the United States.

young people download music from the Internet onto their personal computers. Popular types of music include electronica, rap, and a type of Algerian pop music called *raï*.

raï
rye

For their television viewing pleasure, teens can tune in to both public channels and cable channels. Public channels are general-interest stations with news, cartoons, game shows, documentaries, and French and foreign films. Cable channels offer a music video channel, a foreign movie channel, a French movie channel, and some popular American series such as *Friends, NYPD Blue,* and *The Sopranos.*

Cover to Cover

Reading is another leisurely escape. Teens enjoy French magazines, such as *Paris Match,* a weekly magazine that reports celebrity gossip as well as headline news. *Elle* and *Marie Claire* are other popular choices, especially with teen girls.

Some books that are popular with teen readers are J.K. Rowling's Harry Potter series, the Goosebumps series, and Flavia Bujor's *The Prophecy of the Stones.* Comic books are considered

A French bookseller bares an amazing resemblance to Harry Potter when in costume. He holds a copy of Harry Potter and the Half Blood Prince.

a very serious form of art, with comic book authors who cater to both children and adult readers. The sale of comics and graphic novels has been breaking records since 2004. In that year, five out of the 10 best-selling books in France were graphic novels.

Active Bodies

France has been described as a nation of sports enthusiasts, and two-thirds of the population regularly take part in athletic activities. While in the past, the French have been known for their academic achievements rather than

Kayaking is a popular pastime on the Gave d'Oloron river in south-western France.

The Stade de France at Saint-Denis can hold 80,000 football (soccer) fans.

their athletic success, today the country is known for many athletic achievements as well.

French teenagers often pursue fitness hobbies that include working out in a gym, playing a team sport, cycling, downhill skiing, kayaking, and swimming. They are concerned with their body image and strive for healthy, fit bodies. Most young people are members of a sports association because there are no sports offered through the public school system. Enrolling in sports such as tennis, football (soccer), swimming, and skiing is a good way to make friends.

In the spring, many teens can be found playing football. The French are extremely enthusiastic about football, which is one of their international sports. Teens enjoy watching football on television. The French watch an average of 500 hours of football a year on television.

The professional French football team is nicknamed Les Bleus. European clubs are allowed to field as many European players as they want, so French players often leave to play for more money in Italy, Spain, Britain, and Germany. In 2001, Zinedine Zidane, known as Zizou by French fans, went to the Real Madrid team for

53,900,848 euros (U.S.$64.45 million), making him the most expensive player in football history at that time.

In southwestern France, rugby is the most popular spectator sport. The European rugby competition, called le Tournoi des Six Nations, is played with the hopes of winning for national pride. England, France, Ireland, Italy, Scotland, and Wales all participate. Another rugby competition, the World Cup, includes these six European nations along with Australia, New Zealand, and Fiji.

Each year, France almost comes

Zizou! Zizou!

Zinedine Zidane became world famous following his ejection from the 2006 World Cup finals after head butting another player in the chest. However, he's been a household name in France for far longer.

Zidane was born on June 23, 1972, in Marseille to Algerian immigrants. He joined his first professional football team at the age of 16, and quickly worked his way up to Juventus Turin, one of the most successful football clubs in the world. He attracted international attention during the 1998 World Cup final by heading two goals, giving his team its first FIFA World Cup title. Individually, he has won every major award a player can receive in professional football, including FIFA World Player of the Year three times and European Football Player of the Year in 1998. He is also well-known for his support of charities, giving money and volunteering his own time.

ACTIVE MINDS, ACTIVE BODIES

During the Tour de France, participants consume and burn as many as 10,000 calories per day.

to a halt during the Tour de France, a world-famous bicycle race. French journalist and cyclist Henri Desgrange created the Tour de France in 1903 to promote his new sports newspaper. Except for the summers during World War I and World War II, the race has been held every year since.

The 2,000-plus mile (3,200 km) race features 21 teams of nine riders each and attracts the world's top cyclists. Although the race takes a different route around the country each year, it always includes a trek through the Alps and the Pyrénées mountains and finishes in Paris on the Champs-Elysées. The race, which attracts 15 million spectators annually, begins in late June and lasts three weeks. France's own Bernard Hinault has won five times, and American Lance Armstrong has won seven times.

Mountain biking is another activity that teens enjoy watching and doing. Frenchman Christian Taillefer holds the world's speed record on a mountain bike: He rode down a snow-covered slope at 131 miles (212 km) per hour.

Looking Ahead

THE FRENCH TEENS OF TODAY STRIVE TO SUCCEED IN THE RIGOROUS EDUCATIONAL SYSTEM WITH THE HOPE THAT ONE DAY THEY WILL CONTRIBUTE TO THE FINE PRODUCTS AND SERVICES FOR WHICH FRANCE IS KNOWN. In addition to dealing with the challenges of high-pressure academics, teens in France are living in a climate of cultural tension. The pride of country and tradition is firmly rooted in the mind-set of native French people, and some are uncertain how immigrants and their children fit in.

As they look toward adulthood, French youth will be faced with the challenge of hanging on to the traditional beliefs that the French lifestyle holds, while embracing the changes that are affecting their country.

At a Glance

Official name: French Republic

Capital: Paris

People

Population: 60,876,136

Population by age group:
0–14 years: 18.3%
15–64 years: 65.3%
65 and up: 16.4%

Life expectancy at birth: 79.73 years

Official language: French

Religion:
Roman Catholic: 83%
Muslim: 10%
Protestant: 2%
Jewish: 1%
Unaffiliated: 4%

Legal ages:
Alcohol Consumption: 16
Driver's license: 18
Marriage: 18
Military service: 17
Voting: 18

Government

Type of government: Republic

Chief of state: President, elected by popular vote

Head of government: Prime Minister, nominated by the Assemblée Nationale (National Assembly) majority and appointed by the president

Lawmaking body: Parlement (Parliament), consists of the Sénat (Senate) and Assemblée Nationale (National Assembly)

Administrative divisions: 22 regions

National symbols:
National bird: Gallic rooster
National flower: Lily

Geography

Total Area: 218,812 square miles (547,030 sq km)

Climate:
Atlantic climate: Affects the north with misty, wet conditions
Continental climate: Affects central and eastern France with dry, cold winters; hot, dry summers; and rainy periods in spring and fall
Mediterranean climate: Affects south with hot, dry summers and mild winters

Highest point: Mont Blanc, 15,863 feet (4,807 meters)

Lowest point: Rhone River delta, 6 ½ feet (2 meters) below sea level

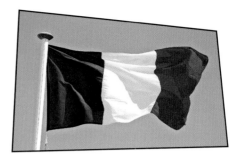

Major landforms: French Alps, Jura Mountains, Paris Basin, Pyrénées Mountains, Rhone River delta

Major rivers: Seine, Rhone, Loire, Garonne

Economy

Currency: Euro

Population below poverty line: 6.5%

Major natural resources: Coal, iron ore, bauxite, fish, timber, zinc

Major agricultural products: Wheat, cereals, sugar beets, potatoes, wine grapes, beef, dairy, fish

Major exports: Machinery, transportation equipment, chemicals, iron and steel products, agricultural products, textiles, clothing

Major imports: Crude oil, machinery and equipment, chemicals, agricultural products

Historical Timeline

 Charlemagne
is crowned emperor of
the Holy Roman Empire

 Martin Luther posts his
95 Theses, beginning the
Protestant Reformation
in Germany

 The Maya rise to
prominence in
Central America

Bubonic plague begins
to sweep through
Europe, killing more
than 25 million people

| 1000–750 B.C. | A.D. 250 | 400 | 800 | 1066 | 1347 | 1453 | 1517 | 1600s |

The Franks settle
in France

Normandy's William
the Conqueror defeats
the Anglo-Saxon
army in the Battle
of Hastings

British colonies
are established
in North America

Celtic tribes migrate
from Central Europe
to France

King Charles VII
forces the English
out of France

 Historical World Event

Napoleon's army is defeated at the Battle of Waterloo in Belgium, and Napoleon is exiled

The French Revolution begins with a mob storming the Bastille prison in Paris

France sells the Louisiana Territory, essentially doubling the size of the United States

France fights England in the Seven Years' War

| 1643–1715 | 1756–1763 | 1769 | 1789 | 1793 | 1799 | 1803 | 1815 |

James Watt patents the steam engine, initiating the Industrial Revolution

Napoléon Bonaparte seizes power; he becomes emperor in 1804

Louis XIV rules France, establishing the country's boundaries, which remain today

King Louis XVI and his wife, Marie Antoinette, are executed

Historical Timeline

New youth employment laws spark mass demonstrations throughout France; a new law is drafted

France is liberated from Nazi control following the Battle of Normandy

 World War I

Jacques Chirac is elected president, ending a 14-year Socialist presidency; he is re-elected in 2002

| 1889 | 1914–1918 | 1939–1945 | 1944 | 1991 | 1994 | 1995 | 2002 | 2006 |

The Eiffel Tower is built for the International Exposition of Paris

 Soviet Union collapses

A single European currency, the euro, replaces the franc

 World War II

The Channel Tunnel opens, linking France and England by rail under the English Channel

Glossary

assimilate	to become familiar with and fit in to the culture of another population or group
contemporaries	people who are about the same age
denominational	related to a particular religion
etiquette	the conduct required by social convention or authority
European Union	an organization of 25 European countries, including France, that runs a single economic market and currency
infantry	soldiers who fight on foot
logic	the study of the rules of reasoning
monarchy	type of government in which a king or queen is the head of state
Renaissance	period in Europe beginning in the 14th century and ending in mid-17th century that is noted for its cultural achievements
republic	government in which leaders are elected by the people to represent them
subsidized	having partial financial support from a government
topography	shapes and forms of land in a particular area; includes mountains, valleys, plains, lakes, and rivers

Additional Resources

IN THE LIBRARY

Connolly, Sean. *The French Revolution*. Chicago: Heinemann, 2003.

Hoben, Sarah. *Daily Life in Ancient and Modern Paris*. Minneapolis: Runestone Press, 2001.

Malone, Margaret Gay. *France*. Tarrytown, N.Y.: Benchmark Books, 2003.

Nardo, Don. *France*. New York: Children's Press, 2000.

Parks, Peggy J. *Foods of France*. Detroit: KidHaven Press, 2006.

Sommers, Michael A. *France: A Primary Source Cultural Guide*. New York: PowerPlus Books, 2005.

Look for more Global Connections books.

Teens in Australia

Teens in Brazil

Teens in China

Teens in India

Teens in Israel

Teens in Japan

Teens in Kenya

Teens in Mexico

Teens in Russia

Teens in Saudi Arabia

Teens in Spain

Teens in Venezuela

Teens in Vietnam

ON THE WEB

For more information on this topic, use FactHound.

1. Go to *www.facthound.com*

2. Type in this book ID: 0756520622

3. Click on the *Fetch It* button.

Source Notes

Page 14, column 1, line 1: Linda Kush. "French Teens Adjust to the New World." *Tewksbury Advocate.* 20 April 2006. www2.townonline.com/tewksbury/localRegional/view.bg?articleid=476877

Page 14, column 1, line 10: Embassy of France, Washington, D.C. "Education in France: The School System," 2005. 27 July 2006. www.ambafrance-us.org/atoz/edu_fr.asp

Page 18, column 1, line 8: Kimberly Conniff Taber. "Isolation Awaits French Girls in Headscarves." *Women's eNews.* 5 March 2004. 27 July 2006. www.womensenews.org/article.cfm/dyn/aid/1738

Page 28, column 1, line 9: Dimitri Naissant. "Virtual Journey of France: Daily Life." Oxfam's Cool Planet. 27 July 2006. www.oxfam.org.uk/coolplanet/ontheline/explore/journey/france/daylife1.htm

Page 32, column 1, line 13: Ibid.

Page 32, sidebar, column 1, line 2: Ibid.

Page 37, column 1, line 6: Caroline Wyatt. "France Boosts Family Incentives." BBC News, 23 Sept. 2005. 27 July 2006. http://news.bbc.co.uk/2/hi/europe/4274200.stm

Page 39, column 2, line 9: John Leicester. "France Seeks to Boost Fertility Rate." *Deseret News.* 22 Sept. 2005. 9 Aug. 2006. www.findarticles.com/p/articles/mi_qn4188/is_20050922/ai_n15623604

Page 43, sidebar, column 2, line 9: Mary Papenfuss. "French Youths Speaking Their Own Language." *USA Today Online.* 5 Jan. 2006. 2 Feb. 2006. www.usatoday.com/news/world/2006-01-05-french.slang x.htm

Page 51, column 1, line 3: Christian Dupavillon. Embassy of France, Washington, D.C. "Fête de la Musique: Annual Street Music Festival," 2005. 2 Aug. 2006. www.ambafrance-us.org/atoz/fet_mus.asp

Page 59, column 1, line 12: "French Teens Adjust to the New World."

Pages 84-85: At a Glance: United States. Central Intelligence Agency. *The World Factbook—France.* 2 Nov. 2006. 6 Nov. 2006. www.cia.gov/cia/publications/factbook/geos/fr.html

Select Bibliography

Dépinoy, Denis. Personal interview. 21 Nov. 2005.

Dupavillon, Christian. Embassy of France, Washington, D.C. "Fête de la Musique: Annual Street Music Festival," 2005. 2 Aug. 2006. www.ambafrance-us.org/atoz/fet_mus.asp

Embassy of France, Washington, D.C. "Education in France: The School System," 2005. 27 July 2006. www.ambafrance-us.org/atoz/edu_fr.asp

Embassy of France, Washington, D.C. "Family Policy in France," 16 Jan. 2001. 6 Nov. 2006. www.ambafrance-us.org/atoz/fam_pol.asp

Fetzer, Joel, and Christopher Soper. *Muslims and the State in Britain, France, and Germany.* New York: Cambridge University Press, 2005.

French Republic. French Ministry of Foreign Affairs. 6 Nov. 2006. www.diplomatie.gouv.fr/en/

Kush, Linda. "French Teens Adjust to the New World." *Tewksbury Advocate.* 20 April 2006. www2.townonline.com/tewksbury/localRegional/view.bg?articleid=476877

Leicester, John. "France Seeks to Boost Fertility Rate." *Deseret News.* 22 Sept. 2005. 9 Aug. 2006. www.findarticles.com/p/articles/mi_qn4188/is_20050922/ai_n15623604

Naissant, Dimitri. "Virtual Journey of France: Daily Life." Oxfam's Cool Planet. 27 July 2006. www.oxfam.org.uk/coolplanet/ontheline/explore/journey/france/daylife1.htm

Papenfuss, Mary. "French Youths Speaking Their Own Language." *USA Today Online.* 5 Jan. 2006. 2 Feb. 2006. www.usatoday.com/news/world/2006-01-05-french.slang x.htm

Rosenberg, Dan. "Rai Rebel." *Metro Times*. 10 July 2001. 6 Nov. 2006. www.metrotimes.com/editorial/story.asp?id=2022

Ross, Steele. *When In France, Do As the French Do*. New York: McGraw-Hill, 2002.

Ruck, Adam. *Foder's Exploring France*. New York: Random House, 2005.

Taber, Kimberly Conniff. "Isolation Awaits French Girls in Headscarves." *Women's eNews*. 5 March 2004. 27 July 2006. www.womensenews.org/article.cfm/dyn/aid/1738

Tomalin, Barry. *Culture Smart! France*. Portland, Ore.: Graphic Arts Center Publishing, 2003.

Turner, Barry. *France Profiled*. New York: St. Martin's Press, 1999.

United States. Central Intelligence Agency. *The World Factbook—France*. 2 Nov. 2006. 6 Nov. 2006. www.cia.gov/cia/publications/factbook/geos/fr.html

Wyatt, Caroline. "France Boosts Family Incentives." BBC News. 23 Sept. 2005. 27 July 2006. http://news.bbc.co.uk/2/hi/europe/4274200.stm

Index

About the Author
Nickie Kranz

Nickie Kranz teaches English composition courses at Minnesota State University, Mankato. She is currently pursuing her M.A. degree in literature. Her two favorite pastimes are reading literature from the Middle Ages and cooking. Nickie lives in the Mankato area with her husband, Luke, and her two sons, Judd and Zane. They enjoy traveling, hiking, four-wheeling, and downhill skiing.

About the Content Adviser
Jean-Philippe Mathy, Ph.D.

A published author himself, Jean-Philippe Mathy served as our content adviser for *Teens in France*. Some of his research and teaching interests include French literature and civilization and modern French and European intellectual history. Dr. Mathy is currently a professor in the Department of French at the University of Illinois at Urbana-Champaign.